SHORT WALK

C000054080

Wiltshire
Pubs

Nigel Vile

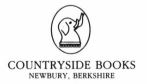

COUNTRYSIDE BOOKS
NEWBURY, BERKSHIRE

First Published 1995
© Nigel Vile 1995

All rights reserved. No reproduction
permitted without the prior permission
of the publishers:

COUNTRYSIDE BOOKS
3 Catherine Road
Newbury, Berkshire

ISBN 1 85306 371 1

Designed by Mon Mohan
Cover illustration by Colin Doggett
Photographs by the author
Maps by Gill Vile

Produced through MRM Associates Ltd., Reading
Typeset by Paragon Typesetters, Queensferry, Clwyd
Printed by Woolnough Bookbinding Ltd., Irthlingborough

Contents

Area map showing locations of the walks.

Publisher's Note

We hope that you obtain considerable enjoyment from this book; great care has been taken in its preparation. However, changes of landlord and actual closures are sadly not uncommon. Likewise, although at the time of publication all routes followed public rights of way or permitted paths, diversion orders can be made and permissions withdrawn.

We cannot of course be held responsible for such diversion orders and any inaccuracies in the text which result from these or any other changes to the routes, nor any damage which might result from walkers trespassing on private property. However, we are anxious that all details covering the walks and the pubs are kept up to date and would therefore welcome information from readers which would be relevant to future editions.

Introduction

If you enjoy peace and solitude, Wiltshire is an ideal county. The majority of tourists simply pass by, on their way to the crowded beaches of Devon, Cornwall and the South Coast, with little more than a cursory glance at the landscape. Apart from the vastly overrated pile of stones at Stonehenge, nowadays totally overwhelmed by coach parties of visitors, Wiltshire is a little-known and infrequently explored county. Its real asset for the walker is that few tourists come to stay, which means that you can have a peaceful and relaxed day out in the countryside. In one sense this is surprising, since we have here scenery that is, arguably, unrivalled in southern England. The local landscape can match anything to be found on the North or South Downs, for example, but without the hordes that throng Box Hill or Leith Hill in Surrey on a summer's weekend.

Each walk is centred on one of the many historic inns that grace the Wiltshire landscape. The aim is to provide as rich a variety of watering holes as is possible. This means that, alongside traditional freehouses and the pubs owned by smaller independent brewers, you will find inns that belong to large nationwide chains. A pen portrait of each pub is provided – its history, its character, the food on offer and the range of beers and ales available.

Generally speaking, most pubs should be open at lunchtimes between 11.30 am and 2.30 pm, with food being available between 12 noon and 2 pm. Equally, in the evenings you can expect the opening hours to extend from 6 pm to 10.30 pm, with food available from around 7 pm. However, pub opening hours are the subject of constant change and variation, depending upon demand, seasonal factors and occasionally the whim of the landlord. Therefore, rather than specify opening hours in each case, only to be proven wrong by the time the book goes to print, each pub's telephone number is included should you wish to make a precise enquiry. Most pubs display their opening hours at their main entrance, enabling this information to be obtained before you set off on your walk.

The walks are deliberately of modest length, making them

suitable for all kinds of walkers from the more mature person to the typical family. Each should provide a morning or an afternoon of exercise and interest, which can be followed by a relaxing meal and a drink in the relevant pub. Whilst the directions and sketch maps in the book are adequate for route-finding – compasses won't be needed in this part of the world! – it is better for the walker to back this up with an Ordnance Survey map. The appropriate OS Landranger sheet, 1:50 000, is specified for each walk, and should be as much a part of your equipment as the obligatory waterproof clothing and stout footwear.

Parking should be done with due consideration. If you intend to visit the pub following the walk, then it is only common courtesy to seek the landlord's permission prior to leaving your vehicle in his empty car park in the morning. On most occasions, landlords are only too happy to oblige. If you are doing a walk and not visiting the pub, then you have no right to use the car park. Whatever the circumstances, in nearly every case I have indicated alternative parking arrangements in the vicinity of each pub.

At the end of your walk, you could well be hot and sticky, damp and muddy. It is only polite, therefore, to both the landlord and his other customers if you attempt some form of wash and brush-up after your walk. If nothing else, at least leave muddy walking boots in your car.

I hope that this book will bring you many hours of pleasure. Not only do these walks open up the Wiltshire countryside, they also introduce some of the finest inns and public houses in the county. I wish you many happy hours of walking.

Nigel A. Vile
Spring 1995

Malmesbury
The Smoking Dog

1

The ancient borough of Malmesbury grew up as a hilltop town, almost on an island formed by tributary branches of the river Avon. The High Street runs down from the magnificent abbey to St John's Bridge and the river, passing en route the delightfully named Smoking Dog. The inn fronts onto the road, sandwiched between the terraced cottages that line the High Street. The profusion of Cotswold stone is a reminder of the influence of neighbouring Gloucestershire in this part of the county.

Wooden floors, exposed stone and traditional beams lend a rustic feel to the bar area, with pine furniture and a large open fireplace completing the decor. A passageway leads through to the dining room, where meals can be enjoyed in a quiet, relaxed atmosphere away from the lively conversation 'out front'. To the rear of the Smoking Dog, a small garden is popular in the summer months.

The inn has quite rightly earned a fine reputation for its ever-changing selection of fine food. The main menu always lists a number of imaginative options, such as courgette, mushroom and pepper-filled pancakes or a duo of sausage kebabs, char-grilled with spicy tomato sauce. Lesser appetites might prefer one of the excellent baguettes on offer, or simply a bowl of Breton onion soup. It is good, too, to see that youngsters are not overlooked. Those hardy annuals – sausages, fish fingers, burgers and chips – will certainly keep most children happy. Real ale enthusiasts will not leave the Smoking Dog disappointed, either. Fuller's, Spitfire, Smiles, Archers, Wadworth 6X, Old Peculier... and even a house-brew called Doggers Bitter! Don't expect the full range of beers on every visit – just a selection. There is a board in the bar, however, where future beers and ales booked to appear are listed. This makes a return visit seem almost obligatory and it comes as no surprise to see the description included in one local pub guide – 'a beer drinker's paradise'.

Telephone: 01666 825823.

How to get there: Malmesbury lies 10 miles north of Chippenham, on the A429 Cirencester road. If you approach the town from the south, leave the A429 at the first roundabout and follow the 'Town Centre' turning. This road crosses the Avon at St John's Bridge, and in just 200 yards you will pass the Smoking Dog at the lower end of the High Street.

Parking: There is no car park at the Smoking Dog, and parking on the roadside opposite is only permitted for 1 hour – Sundays excepted. Some 150 yards south of the inn, you can park in St John's Street alongside the Rose and Crown for up to 23 hours. This should give you ample time to complete the walk!

Length of the walk: 1½ miles. Map: OS Landranger 173 Swindon and Devizes (inn GR 934870).

Alfred the Great granted Malmesbury a charter in AD 880, making it England's oldest borough. History is everywhere in the town, with the ancient abbey being but the jewel in the crown. The market cross dating from 1490, almshouses dating from the 17th century and a former four-storey cloth mill also lie along the route. The mill reminds us that Malmesbury was at one time a thriving weaving centre, with the river Avon powering the local waterwheels. Malmesbury marks the confluence of two of the river's tributaries – the river Avon (Tetbury Branch) and the river Avon (Sherston Branch). Both are followed along the way, their rural location contrasting with the town section of the walk.

The Walk
Head down the High Street until you approach Avon Mill and the river Avon. Just before St John's Bridge, go through a gateway on the right and then turn left to cross a footbridge over the river. Walk a few yards along the road at the far side of the Avon, before turning right through a gate into the

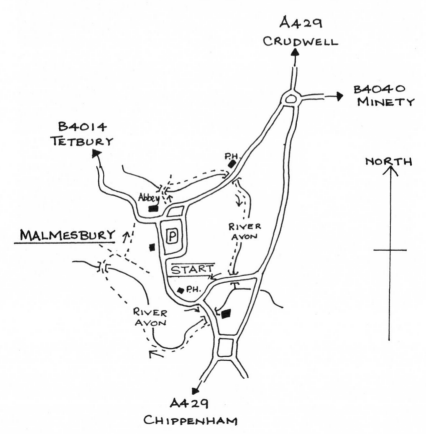

Avon Mill, Malmesbury.

watermeadow. Follow the river upstream for 600 yards –
initially along the river bank, latterly alongside a field boundary
above the river – until you come to a stone footbridge across
the Avon.

Cross this bridge, and a larger footbridge beyond, and
continue the short distance to a lane. Turn right along this lane,
called Burnivale, and pass above the Maltings housing estate,

which lies alongside the Avon. In a short distance, bear left up a flight of steps that climb up to busy Gloucester Street. Turn right, pass the entrance to the abbey (obligatory detour!) and turn left into a side turning immediately past the market cross. This turning runs alongside the Whole Hog restaurant.

In just 25 yards, turn left onto a tarmac footpath that carries a signpost bearing the legend 'Cloisters Garden'. Continue down this footpath as it runs alongside the abbey, but ignore the left turn into the gardens. The path descends a flight of steps, at the foot of which you bear right to cross the Avon. Once across the river, look out for a wooden stile on the right and a path leading into the signposted Conygre Mead nature reserve. A gravel path passes through woodland, before following the river bank through to the B4040 and the Duke of York.

Turn right at the road, cross the Avon and immediately bear left along the signposted path that runs through the watermeadows by the river. This well-worn path crosses two fields to reach a wooden footbridge. At the road junction beyond the bridge, turn right and you will find yourself in St John's Street. The road soon reaches the Lower High Street by St John's Almshouses, where a right turn will bring you back to the Smoking Dog.

② **Ashton Keynes**
The Horse and Jockey

Ashton Keynes lies on the northern edge of Wiltshire, just a mile or two from the Gloucestershire border at South Cerney. The influence of the neighbouring county is everywhere, with Cotswold limestone having been used in the construction of all the older properties in the village. The inn itself is thought to date from the 16th century, and was originally a pair of cottages.

The two bars and the family room are comfortably furnished with dark wood table-and-chair sets, pine settles and cushioned sofas. Exposed stonework and original beams add to the traditional feel of the inn. Living up to its name, a collection of racing prints adorn the walls of the Horse and Jockey, where sharp eyes will also spot a display case of jockey tags and a fox's head. On sunny days, food and drink can be enjoyed in the inn's garden and a play area is provided.

The racing theme is continued on the menu, where the courses are described as Starters, Gallops and Finishing Post. Amongst the Starters, garlic mushrooms or peppered mackerel would tempt most palates, whilst Cumberland sausage or a barbecued half-rack of ribs or half a roast duck might appeal from the Gallops. If your appetite stretches as far as the Finishing Post selections, spotted dick or pineapple surprise might prove enticing options. Vegetarians are catered for with dishes such as cauliflower cheese and vegetable Mexicana, whilst the children's menu includes pizza, beefburger, fish fingers and sausages. Ushers, the Trowbridge-based brewery, own the Horse and Jockey. You could do a lot worse than sample a pint of their Best.

Telephone: 01285 861270.

How to get there: Ashton Keynes is situated north of the B4040 Malmesbury to Cricklade road. Turn onto the B4696 at the traffic lights 1 mile east of Minety. Just as you enter the village, look out for a right turn along a lane marked 'Gosditch'. The inn lies a few yards along this lane, on the right-hand side.

Parking: There is a car park in front of the Horse and Jockey.

Length of the walk: 2½ miles. Map: OS Landranger 163 Cheltenham and Cirencester (inn GR 043939).

Ashton Keynes has a real Cotswold feel, with the local stone being the dominant building material used in the village. The infant Thames flows alongside Church Walk, where fine 18th century houses overlook the clear waters of the river. To the west of the village lies an area of gravel workings. Many of the former excavations have now been flooded to form the Cotswold Water Park. This walk passes alongside half a dozen of the park's lakes.

The Walk

From the inn, continue along Gosditch to the centre of Ashton Keynes. Turn left along the village's main street, and continue past the White Hart for 200 yards until you reach Church Walk. Turn left into this beautiful cul-de-sac, walking alongside the Thames. Cross the river at the bridge, and continue to a gateway. Beyond this gate, a tarmac path leads to Holy Cross church.

Join the B4696 beyond the church, and turn right for 200 yards until you reach a road junction. There is no pavement

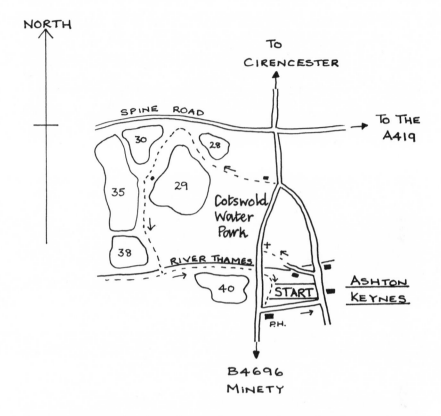

NORTH

To
CIRENCESTER

SPINE ROAD

To THE
A419

30
28

35
29

Cotswold
Water
Park

38

RIVER THAMES

40
START

ASHTON
KEYNES

P.H.

B4696
MINETY

along this stretch of road, so take care! Opposite the turning to Ashton Keynes, cross a stile on the left-hand side, signposted to South Cerney. The path borders a garden fence in the first field – notice the model railway in the garden – before crossing a pair of stiles in the corner. After the second stile, bear left to reach one further stile in the hedgerow at the far side of the next field. The path then continues for a few yards to reach a track on the fringes of the gravel workings.

Turn right along this track, which very soon bears to the left. Continue ahead along the main track as it passes between lakes 28 and 29 of the Cotswold Water Park. In 200 yards, just before the Spine Road, the track sweeps to the left to head back towards Ashton Keynes. Follow the track around to the left, and you will soon find yourself walking between lakes 29 and 30. Beyond an old ruin – Field Barn – the track runs alongside

15

The river Thames at Ashton Keynes.

lake 35 on the right, active gravel workings lying on the left-hand side.

Where lake 35 ends, the track bears to the left to run alongside the eastern edge of lake 38. Our route lies in this direction, but look out for the enclosed path that runs between the track and the lake itself – a better option, given that gravel lorries regularly use the main track. Where lake 38 ends, the path continues into a belt of trees where a footbridge crosses the Thames. Once across the bridge, turn left to follow the riverside path for 400 yards back to the B4696.

Turn right for just 10 yards before crossing a low metal stile on the other side of the road, into the enclosure containing the Ashton Keynes Pumping Station. Turn right and follow a field path that runs parallel to the road through three fields. It rejoins the main road in 200 yards, where you continue along the pavement for a short distance to the first turning on the left. This is Gosditch, and the Horse and Jockey lies just along the road.

3 Coate
The Sun Inn

The Sun Inn is a busy roadside hostelry on the main road leading from Swindon to the M4 motorway. This is part of the Arkell's empire, a local brewery founded in Swindon back in 1843. The early growth of the brewery was very much tied in with the expansion of the local railway industry, with Arkell's beers being a favourite tipple of the railway workers.

The inn reflects the local building materials, being a mixture of brick, plaster and timber. It is an imposing structure that has long since changed from a local alehouse to a food-based inn for passing traffic. Internally, the Sun has been extensively modernised to give a warm and comfortable atmosphere. The bar areas are carpeted throughout, and are decorated with patterned wallpaper and floral curtains. Dark wood tables and cushioned chairs, prints and wooden partitions complete the decor.

The usual range of pub food is available, with menu selections covering baguettes, jacket potatoes, ploughman's lunches,

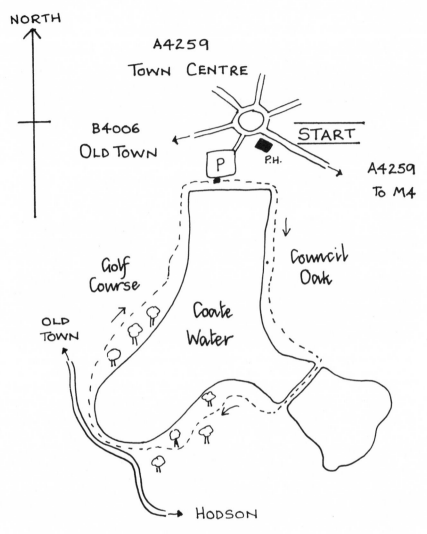

salads, toasted sandwiches, steaks, fish dishes and grills. Vegetarians are offered veggie-burgers, veggie-sausages and vegetarian spring rolls, whilst youngsters will find all their usual favourites. There are light snacks, too, such as peppered mackerel fillet, Japanese-style prawns and chicken dippers. A good selection of sweets are available each day. These might typically include sticky toffee pudding, chocolate sponge and banana split. To accompany your meal, a pint of one of the Arkell's beers comes highly recommended. The choice includes Kingsdown Ale, 2B and 3B. Should the weather be warm, or any youngsters restless, your pint can be enjoyed in the inn's large beer garden. This includes a children's play area as well as an unusual thatched playhouse.

Telephone: 01793 523292.

How to get there: The Coate Water roundabout lies on the A4259, midway between Swindon town centre and junction 15 of the M4 motorway. The Sun Inn enjoys a prominent location alongside the roundabout.

Parking: There is a car park for patrons alongside the Sun. As Coate Water lies very close by, it is a better option to park at the country park rather than monopolise the inn's parking spaces.

Length of the walk: 2 miles. Map: OS Landranger 173 Swindon and Devizes (inn GR 178828).

This short walk explores Coate Water, a man-made lake on the edge of Swindon that was created as a reservoir for the Wiltshire and Berkshire Canal. Richard Jefferies, Wiltshire's best-known country writer, was born in Coate in 1848. He described this stretch of water as a 'weedy mere' – a great injustice to the magnificent country park that has subsequently been created from Coate Water. As you follow the Lakeside Walk, keep your eyes skinned for the rich variety of birdlife that thrives both on the water and in the surrounding woodland. Great crested grebes, grey herons, Canada geese, kingfishers, coots, little owls and lesser spotted woodpeckers are but a selection of the species that can be seen here throughout the year.

The Walk

A driveway leads from the Sun Inn and the Coate Water roundabout down to the Coate Water car park and the warden's centre. Follow the path to the left up to the lakeside, signposted to the picnic area, trains and sandpit. Continue along the eastern side of the lake, past the play area and onto the Council Oak, where a plaque reads, 'Described by Richard Jefferies born at Coate 1849 in his novel Bevis the story of a boy.'

Continue beyond the Council Oak to a causeway that

19

Coate Water.

separates the main stretch of water from a more recent extension. At the far side of this causeway, turn right to follow the signposted 'Lakeside Walk'. This path soon leaves the side of the water to pass through the marshy woodland at the southern end of Coate Water.

When you reach the lane leading to Hodson, turn right and follow the path alongside the road. In 150 yards, just before an information board, turn right to continue along the Lakeside Walk. This next section of the walk has Coate Water hidden behind the trees. There are one or two cul-de-sac paths, however, that give access to the water's edge.

Shortly, the path passes through an avenue of trees beside a golf course before rejoining Coate Water just beyond a yacht compound. It is now a simple matter of following the waterside path back to the end of the lake and the parking area.

Langley Burrell
The Brewery Arms

The Brewery Arms takes its name from a former brewery that stood alongside this village hostelry. Sadly, the brewery is no more. The building now houses the local offices of the National Farmers' Union. The inn has a cottage-style appearance, with its construction of local stone being a reminder that Langley Burrell is on the fringes of the Cotswolds.

The inn has both public and lounge bars, which connect with a comfortably furnished rear dining area. The lounge bar is cosy and intimate, with wooden settles and tables grouped around an open fireplace. Thick beams add a traditional touch to the bar, where dark floral wallpaper decorates not only the walls but also the ceiling. The small bookshelf alongside the fireplace has an appropriate range of reading material that includes both *The Good Beer Guide* and a guide to local ciders. Prints and plates complete the decor.

The menu at the Brewery Arms includes an imaginative range of baguettes, jacket potatoes, toasted sandwiches and ploughman's lunches. The selections also include nachos, walnut and lentil loaf, breaded seafood platter and crispy coated vegetables with a Stilton dip. Each day a range of specials are displayed on the board in the bar, for example, pheasant in a red wine sauce, liver and pork pâté and leek and potato soup. The portions are generous and well-prepared, and represent good value for money. Youngsters are welcome to join their parents in the eating area of the bar. To accompany your meal, two fine Wiltshire beers are available at the inn. Ushers Best Bitter, brewed in Trowbridge, and the excellent Wadworth 6X, from Devizes, should satisfy most palates. Wadworth use a 92% malt mash for their 6X brew, which is produced using the 'partigyle' system. If that sounds too scientific, just rest assured that 6X is a good old-fashioned ale.

Telephone: 01249 652707.

How to get there: Langley Burrell lies just off the B4069 Lyneham road, 1 mile north of Chippenham. Turn off the B4069 onto the signposted road leading into the village, and you will find the Brewery Arms fronting onto the road in just ¼ mile.

Parking: There is a car park for patrons in front of the Brewery Arms, as well as roadside parking in the immediate vicinity of the inn.

Length of the walk: 2½ miles. Map: OS Landranger 173 Swindon and Devizes (inn GR 933752).

From Langley Burrell, our steps follow a section of Maud Heath's Causeway to the neighbouring hamlet of Kellaways. Maud Heath was a market woman from Langley Burrell, who left sufficient capital on her death in 1474 for a dry pathway to be constructed from Wick Hill to the market in Chippenham. Although the path is mainly at road level – indeed, it appears to be little more than a pavement for much of its route – at Kellaways, 60 raised arches carry the path more than 6 ft above road level. This is where Maud Heath's Causeway crosses the river Avon, and the damp meadowland necessitated such a construction. The return to Langley Burrell follows the banks of the Avon, a pleasant riverside walk where ornithologists will discover a rich variety of birdlife and wildfowl.

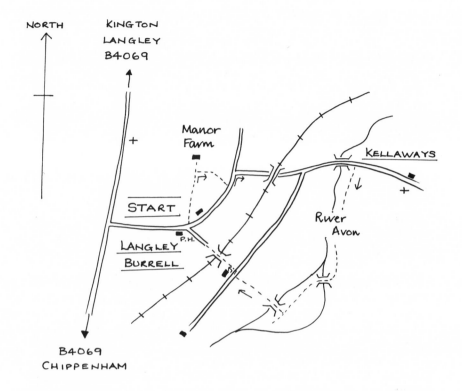

The Walk

From the Brewery Arms, walk 100 yards along the road away from the B4069 in the direction of Kellaways. Take the first turning on the left, signposted to the village hall, and follow this byway for 300 yards to a small tributary stream of the river Avon. Cross this stream and turn immediately to the right to follow the edge of an open field beside the watercourse. Follow the right-hand edge of this field for ¼ mile, all the way to a gate which leads onto the Langley Burrell to Kellaways road.

Cross the road to the pavement opposite – Maud Heath's Causeway – and follow this path to the left for ½ mile into Kellaways. En route, the path passes beneath the main South Wales railway. As soon as you have crossed the Avon, descend the steps on the right down to the river bank – although the detour across the magnificent raised causeway ahead to visit the diminutive St Giles' church is almost obligatory!

Maud Heath's Causeway at Kellaways.

Follow the river bank to the south for almost ¾ mile until you reach a wooden footbridge, in the third field down from the road. Cross this footbridge, and follow the right-hand field boundary in the field beyond for 350 yards before turning right through a gateway. In the next field, follow the left-hand field boundary up to a lane alongside the clearly visible Dolphin Cottage. Turn right at the road and, in just 100 yards, left onto a byway that crosses the main railway line, before continuing into Langley Burrell. Turn left at the main street to return to the Brewery Arms.

At the end of the walk, it is worth heading north for ½ mile on the B4069 to discover St Peter's church. Francis Kilvert, born in nearby Hardenhuish, was curate here in 1863-64 and again in 1872-76.

5 Cherhill
The Black Horse

The village of Cherhill, nestling at the foot of the Wiltshire downs on the Bath Road, seems a fairly law-abiding place nowadays. Things were not always this way, however. Back in the 18th century, the notorious Cherhill Gang stalked the neighbourhood. They were a bunch of marauding highwaymen who, stark naked, would roam the local countryside under cover of darkness! Their base was the local hostelry – the Black Horse. The inn is today altogether more peaceful. Built of local red brick, it serves not only local customers but also travellers from the adjoining A4. The old cart alongside the car park and the plough above the entrance, however, leave visitors in no doubt that Cherhill was historically a farming community. The local downs would have supported any number of shepherds in their heyday.

Although a large part of the Black Horse serves as a restaurant, with the inn having earned a reputation for its food, there is a welcoming bar at the front. With its exposed floorboards,

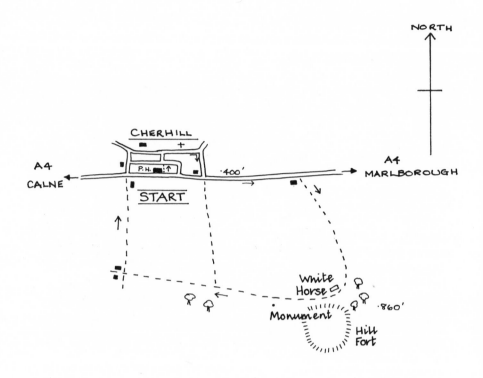

wooden beams, open fireplace and brasses, this area exudes a truly rural atmosphere. In high summer, when patrons wish to relax in the open air, there is a large beer garden to the rear of the Black Horse, with picnic tables, swings and a small aviary. This is an Ushers house, the local Trowbridge-based brewery founded by Thomas Usher back in 1824. Without a doubt, one of their fine beers should be the order of the day. These include Founders, Best Bitter, 1824 Particular and Dark Horse Porter. Accompanying your drink, you can choose from the traditional range of pub food that includes salads and sandwiches, steaks and grills, fish dishes and vegetarian meals.

Telephone: 01249 813365.

How to get there: Cherhill lies 3 miles east of Calne on the A4 heading out towards Marlborough. The Black Horse fronts onto the main road in the middle of the village.

Parking: There is a car park for patrons to the side of the Black Horse. Just 150 yards to the east of the inn, there is also a layby alongside the main road.

Length of the walk: 3 miles. Map: OS Landranger 173 Swindon and Devizes (inn GR 035700).

A stiff climb up to the ramparts of Oldbury Castle, over 800 ft above sea level, brings quite magnificent views across the Wiltshire countryside. Alongside this Iron Age fort lies one of the more famous of Wiltshire's chalk hill figures – the Cherhill White Horse. This was cut in 1780, with its creator, Doctor Christopher Alsop of Calne, shouting instructions to the men on the hillside from the Bath Road! He evidently used some form of primitive megaphone. A further attraction on the hilltop is the Landsdowne Monument. Erected in 1845, this monument commemorates the 17th century political economist Sir William Petty. The route crosses a stretch of typical chalk downland, with close cropped grass and a rich array of flora and fauna. This is a wonderful walk at any time of the year, but in high summer, with the sun beating down, the skylark singing high overhead and the delicate harebell blowing in the gentle breeze, you will see English landscape at its very best.

The Walk

To avoid too much walking alongside the busy A4, the outward route will explore a quiet part of Cherhill that lies just to the north of the main road. This is a circuitous way of reaching the downs, but it is very pleasant. Follow the footpath that runs alongside the Black Horse, signposted to Middle Lane. Cross Middle Lane, and follow the lane opposite down to The Street. Turn right, and continue along The Street and past St James' church, before bearing right into Park Lane. Follow Park Lane up to the A4.

Turn left, and follow the pavement alongside the A4 for ¼ mile until you reach an isolated bungalow on the other side of the road. Turn right alongside this bungalow, follow a track signposted to Oldbury Castle. The track ends at a gate and cattle grid, beyond which you enter National Trust property which includes the hill fort and the surrounding downland. Follow the path up the hillside on the left, towards the beech copse high on the hilltop. The path continues above the Cherhill White

27

St James's church, Cherhill.

Horse and on to the Landsdowne Monument. You will undoubtedly pause for breath somewhere along the way... which will provide the opportunity to enjoy some stunning views across North Wiltshire.

Follow the path to the right of the monument, keeping to the edge of the hilltop. In 200 yards, keep to the right of a hillock and continue on to a collection of gates and stiles. Ignore the chalk track that bears right to head downhill to the A4. Rather, pass through the gates and continue straight ahead across the hilltop field, keeping to the right of the small beech copse. Continue across the hilltop pasture until you reach a track that leads down to the bottom right-hand corner of the field. Here you will find a stile and a National Trust sign.

Continue along the bridlepath beyond this stile for just under ½ mile to a cross-track beside a complex of farm buildings. Turn right, and follow the bridlepath back down into Cherhill and the A4.

You can simply turn right and follow the main road back to the Black Horse, but a quieter option is to cross the road, and head down Olivers Hill. Turn into the second turning on the right – The Street – and in 200 yards turn right to retrace the route followed at the outset, back up to Middle Lane and the Black Horse.

⑥ Avebury
The Red Lion

The Red Lion is arguably the only pub in the country that can claim to lie within the confines of a stone circle, a claim that is justifiably used by the inn to market its overnight accommodation! It is not just the location that makes the Red Lion so appealing, however. This half-timbered hostelry, with a magnificent thatched roof, is one of the most handsome inns in the area. Internally it has been the subject of much modernisation and renovation, with a large restaurant extension. The original bar continues to exude a cosy and intimate charm. Winter months see a roaring log fire in the open fireplace, providing the perfect welcome following a walk across the surrounding open countryside. The bar is furnished with cushioned seats and stools, and circular tables, whilst stonework, plaster and beams provide a reminder as to the inn's historic origins. Around the bar are displayed a number of local prints, as well as old cider pots, china hot-water bottles and a number of copper artefacts. Above the fireplace there is a case of old gas mantles and wicks, a most unusual exhibit. The day's menu is chalked up behind the servery in the restaurant area. The range of dishes changes regularly, with recent selections including pheasant and vegetable pie, lamb chops, faggots, lasagne, various salads and ploughman's lunches. There is always a good range of sweets, with options such as jam roly poly pudding designed to restore those calories lost on the walk. In the evening, the Red Lion offers its 'Twilight Menu'. This contains a number of local themes, including Solstice Salads, Great Barn Pies, Neolithic Snacks and a Crop Circle of Vegetarian Dishes. The pies look especially appealing, and include fish, steak in ale and pork in cider.

The Red Lion is a Whitbread hostelry, which means that brews such as West Country Pale Ale and Winter Royal are usually available. Beyond this, there is a good selection of beers, including Morland's Old Speckled Hen, Boddingtons Bitter and Wadworth 6X. In the summer there are a number of tables outside. This is an impressive inn, very popular with the area's many visitors.

Telephone: 01625 39266.

Stone circle at Avebury.

How to get there: Avebury lies on the A4361, midway between Swindon and Devizes. The Red Lion is situated alongside the main road in the heart of the village – simply keep your eyes open for the magnificent half-timbered, thatched building.

Parking: There is a car park for patrons beside the Red Lion, whilst just a short distance down the High Street – the lane leading from the main road to Avebury village – there is a free car park for visitors.

Length of the walk: 4 miles. Map: OS Landranger 173 Swindon and Devizes (inn GR 102699).

Avebury lies at the heart of perhaps the greatest archaeological centre in Britain. The imprints of ancient civilisation are everywhere in this part of Wiltshire – stone circles, long barrows, round barrows, unexplained mounds and lonely standing stones. This quite exceptional walk includes all of these elements. Beyond the stone circle at Avebury, our steps pass Silbury Hill, West Kennett Long Barrow and the West Kennett Stone Avenue. These ancient relics stand amidst a quite delightful natural landscape, with the infant river Kennet cutting a course across the rolling downland of North Wessex. Fascinating at any time of year, this walk is especially memorable on a crisp midwinter morning. The light and the stillness at that time of year lend a unique feel to this ancient landscape.

The Walk
From the Red Lion, walk down the High Street for about 100 yards before turning off onto an enclosed footpath on the left-hand side. This path runs alongside the ditch and embankment of the stone circle. Follow this path for about 200 yards to the main visitors' car park on the edge of Avebury. Leave the car park, turn right along the A4361 for just a few yards before turning left onto a bridlepath signposted to West Kennett Long Barrow.

This path is followed for ½ mile beside the infant river Kennet to a junction alongside an ancient stone footbridge. Continue ahead at this point, keeping to the left-hand bank of the river. In 200 yards, where the enclosed footpath ends, continue along the edge of the field ahead to the A4. Throughout this section of the walk, there are fine views to the right of Silbury Hill.

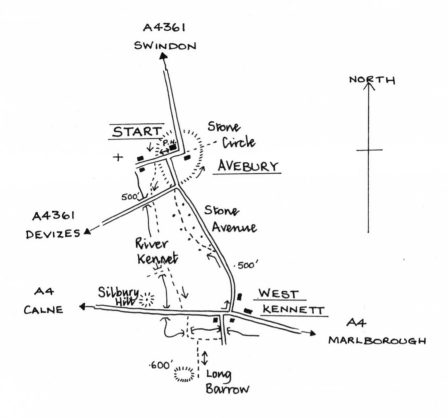

Turn left along the A4 for just a few yards, before turning right onto the signposted footpath leading to the long barrow. This well-defined path crosses the field to the Kennet, beyond which the path follows an enclosed course to West Kennett Long Barrow, high on the hilltop. This is a magical spot, where you will undoubtedly spend time exploring the barrow's interior.

Retrace your steps back down the hill, only this time, where the path bears left, pass through the gap into the field on your right. Walk alongside the bottom edge of this field to the opposite corner, where a track leads down to a quiet lane. Follow this lane to the left, across the Kennet and up to the A4 in West Kennett village. Turn right along the main road – take care no pavement – before turning left in just 200 yards onto

33

the unsignposted B4003 that heads back to Avebury. Following ½ mile of road walking, turn left through the gateway that leads into the enclosure containing the stones that form the West Kennett Stone Avenue.

Follow the Avenue back into Avebury where, at the end of the enclosure, a gate brings you back onto the B4003. Across the road is another gateway. Pass through this to gain access to the embankment that surrounds the Avebury Stone Circle. Follow this embankment all the way to Avebury, crossing a bridlepath and the A4361 en route. Back in Avebury, a flight of steps leads down to a lane that returns to the High Street.

⑦ Ramsbury
The Bell

Ramsbury has a certain ecclesiastical tradition, having been a bishopric between AD 908 and 1058. The village was at that time the seat of the Bishops of Wiltshire, until a succeeding bishop took a liking for Sherborne. Within the present church building there is still evidence of the former Saxon church. At the eastern end of the High Street stood the famous Ramsbury elm. The tree was a seedling at the time of Charles I, whilst nearly 130 years later it provided shelter for the itinerant evangelist John Wesley. Sadly, the massive stump of the tree was removed in 1986, the victim of Dutch elm disease. In its place was planted a semi-mature oak. The Ramsbury elm would have witnessed many events in the life of the village, including the construction of the neighbouring Bell Inn way back in the 17th century.

Originally a coaching inn, the Bell today attracts visitors from a wide area, on account of its well deserved reputation for good food and drink. The bar area is divided up by a massive chimney breast, into which are set a pair of open fireplaces. With its original beams, brick and stone work, the building does indeed convey a real sense of history. Around the walls hang a delightful selection of paintings and sketches, with polished tables and fresh flowers providing a welcoming touch for patrons.

An excellent selection of well-prepared food is available. Home-made soup or pâté are amongst the starters, with the main courses including such tempting dishes as Sussex smokie pie, beef and ale pie, a trio of local sausages with bubble and squeak, and Cajun chicken. A range of daily specials are also available, displaying the inn's catering at its very best. If you can manage a sweet, how about hot apple strudel or sticky walnut and maple sponge? Real ale enthusiasts will also enjoy a visit to the Bell. With Wadworth 6X and IPA, Hook Norton Best Bitter and a guest beer such as Tanglefoot available, drinkers really are spoiled for choice.

Telephone: 01672 20230.

The entrance lodge at Ramsbury Manor.

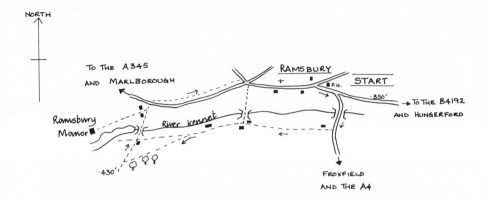

How to get there: Follow the A345 Swindon road out of Marlborough's town centre. In 200 yards, turn right onto an unclassified road leading to Mildenhall and Axford. Ramsbury lies on this road, 3 miles beyond Axford. You will find the Bell at the eastern end of Ramsbury's main street.

Parking: There is ample roadside parking in the vicinity of the Bell, which also has a car park for patrons.

Length of the walk: 2 miles. Map: OS Landranger 174 Newbury and Wantage (inn GR 275716).

This walk explores Ramsbury's main street, as well as the neighbouring Kennet valley. The clear waters of this chalk stream offer fine fishing – access rights are jealously guarded, giving us only tantalising glimpses of the river itself. As an added attraction, our steps pass within sight of Ramsbury Manor. As well as the imposing entrance lodge and gateway, the manor can be glimpsed standing beyond a magnificent tree-lined lake.

The Walk

Follow the Hungerford road, which runs to the right of the Bell. In 100 yards, turn right onto the lane signposted to Froxfield. Cross the Kennet and, in 300 yards, turn right onto a bridlepath signposted to Mill Lane. This enclosed path reaches a pair of thatched cottages in about ½ mile. Just beyond the first cottage, it is worth taking a detour to the right as far as a bridge across

37

the Kennet. This will provide one of the all-too-few glimpses of the river on the walk.

The main walk continues beyond the second cottage to a gateway, beyond which the bridlepath continues to the far left-hand corner of the field. A choice of two paths lies ahead – take the higher enclosed pathway that runs alongside the edge of a hillside field. When this path reaches a hedgerow, cross the stile directly ahead into another open field. Cross this field to the far left-hand corner, with woodland to your left and open views back across Ramsbury.

In the top corner of the field, cross the single-step stile and follow the fence on the right for a few yards down to a wide track. Turn right, and follow this track down to a rank of houses and on across the river Kennet. Away to the left lies Ramsbury Manor, fronting onto a lake created by damming the river. The manor once belonged to Sir William Jones, attorney general to Charles II. Continue along the lane to the road that leads into Ramsbury, passing the entrance gateway to the manor itself.

Across the road from the entrance lodge is a footpath that runs parallel to the road, but separated from it by a hedgerow. Follow this path to the right back into Ramsbury, with the countryside crossed earlier in the walk away to the south. The path rejoins the road on the edge of the village, where you follow the High Street eastwards to return to the Bell.

⑧ Wilton
The Swan Inn

Although off the beaten track, a lot of visitors seek out the tiny village of Wilton on account of two major local attractions – a windmill and a pumping station on the Kennet & Avon Canal. The village, with its brick-and-thatch cottages and duck pond, will not disappoint and the Swan, a brick building dating from the turn of the century, will most certainly add to any visitor's enjoyment of a visit to this corner of Wiltshire.

Internally, there is one spacious bar, with a corner reserved for the pool table. Beams, a wood-burning stove, a grandfather clock and a bookcase add elements of interest to the decor, as do a number of prints, photographs of the local fire brigade in action and a fine selection of brasses. Pine furniture, tables crafted from sewing machine tables, leather-backed chairs and wooden settles complete the furnishings in what, happily, remains very much a local hostelry.

The menu at the Swan covers the traditional range of meals – steaks, chicken dishes, fish, ploughman's lunches, jacket

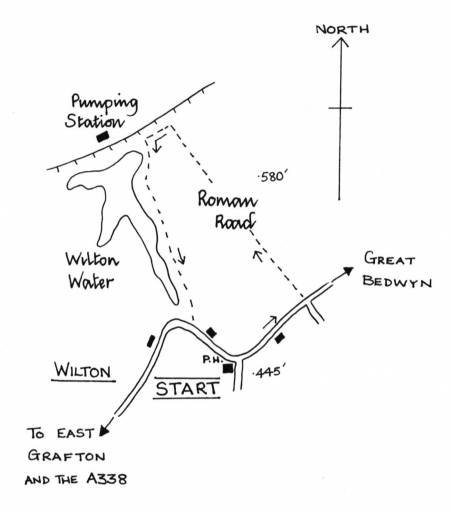

potatoes and sandwiches, as well as more exotic things, like chicken tikka masala with rice, ratatouille with grilled Brie, beef in black bean sauce with rice, and brunch. This last dish is quite amazing and combines Cumberland sausage, bacon, egg, mushrooms, kidney, potatoes, fried bread, beans and tomatoes! A nice touch on the menu is the simple message asking patrons to request anything that isn't listed – it could be possible to prepare the dish in question. That will certainly help parents with fussy youngsters! Real ale enthusiasts will enjoy their visit.

Amongst the beers available are Wadworth 6X, Hook Norton Best Bitter and Foxley Bitter from nearby Mildenhall. Inch's Cider is also on tap. There is a good range of wines, too, the display board listing some delightful tipples.

The Swan has remained a remarkably unspoiled inn over the years. With its sunny garden, its fine village location and the warmth of its welcome, this is a hostelry that you will certainly wish to visit again.

Telephone: 01672 870274.

How to get there: Wilton is signposted from the A338 road south of Hungerford, just 2 miles east of Burbage. The Swan lies in the centre of the village.

Parking: There is a car park for patrons in front of the Swan, and room for careful roadside parking throughout the village.

Length of the walk: 2 miles. Map: OS Landranger 174 Newbury and Wantage (inn GR 268615).

This short walk is never short of interest. From the brick and thatch of Wilton, a section of the Roman road that ran from Cunetio (Mildenhall) to Venta Belgarum (Winchester) takes us over the hilltop and into the neighbouring valley, which carries the Kennet & Avon Canal. A little walk along the towpath brings us to Wilton Water, the summit reservoir that waters this middle section of the canal. The path back to Wilton follows the edge of this stretch of water, where little grebes, Canada geese, mallards and tufted ducks are amongst the regular breeders. An added bonus is the opportunity to visit Crofton Pumping Station, whose Cornish beam engines can still pump water from Wilton Water into the canal.

The Walk

Opposite the Swan is a road junction. Turn left, and follow the lane signposted to Great Bedwyn, out of the village. In ¼ mile, at another junction, where the road forks to Tidcombe, turn left onto a track signposted to Crofton Beam Engines. Follow this track, the old Roman road, as it climbs the hillside before dropping down to the Kennet & Avon Canal.

Follow the towpath to the left, passing lock 61 initially before walking the short distance along to Wilton Water. At this point,

Crofton Pumping Station.

leave the canal and follow the path along the side of the reservoir, signposted to Wilton Windmill.

If you wish to visit the pumping station on the other side of the canal, continue past Wilton Water for a few yards to lock 60, and cross to the far bank, using the plank walkway on the lower lock gates. Follow the footpath under the West of England railway up to the pumping station.

The well-worn path follows the east side of the reservoir all the way back into Wilton, where you emerge onto the village street opposite a duck pond. Turn left, and it is just 100 yards back to the Swan.

9 Oare
The White Hart

Oare enjoys a spectacular location, nestling beneath some fine downland at the eastern end of the Vale of Pewsey. The White Hart sits alongside the main road through the village, the A345 running from Salisbury to Marlborough. This unspoiled village local, a Wadworth house constructed of the local red brick, offers a friendly and comfortable welcome to visitors. The comment in a local pub guide – 'a fine traditional village pub of the best sort' – says it all.

Internally, there are lounge and public bars, whilst to the rear is a pleasant garden with a children's play area. The carpeted lounge is furnished with oak tables and chairs, whilst a number of stools constructed of old tractor seats provide an unusual feature. With the low ceiling, dark beams and brick open fireplace, the White Hart has a definite cottage-like feel. Around the walls hang a variety of prints with rural themes – a country lane and birds of prey, for example – and an old map of Wiltshire will certainly catch the eye of walkers. Brass and

View to the Giant's Grave.

copper artefacts, cider pots, china and flowers complete the picture.

The hills around Oare will certainly give you a healthy appetite! A good selection of bar food is listed on boards in the White Hart. The dishes are wholesome and well-prepared. Starters might include home-made soup or garlic mushrooms, whilst the main meals could be steak and kidney pie, pig in the orchard, homily pie and chicken or ham and leek pie. Steaks, lasagne and fish dishes are also available, along with vegetarian options such as mushroom and nut fetuccine. A range of lighter snacks are also on offer, including ploughman's lunches and delicious filled rolls. The sweets will prove very tempting. These might include home-made apple pie, spotted dick or apricot crumble. To accompany your meal, one of the fine Wadworth beers, 6X or IPA, for example, should be obligatory in this corner of the county. Alternatives would be a pint of Bass, perhaps, or a glass of Beamish.

Telephone: 01672 62273.

How to get there: Oare lies on the A345 Pewsey road, 5 miles south of Marlborough. The White Hart is on the main road in the middle of the village.

Parking: There is a car park for patrons at the White Hart. Roadside parking, with care, can also be found in the side lanes above and below the inn.

Length of the walk: 2 miles. Map: OS Landranger 173 Swindon and Devizes (inn GR 158631).

The village of Oare is set against a quite magnificent backdrop of some of Wiltshire's finest downland. This walk heads up towards Martinsell Hill, where we find the Giant's Grave. Local folklore maintains that the giant will rise from his slumbers if you run seven times around the long barrow containing his earthly remains! Quite apart from that, the views will certainly make you catch your breath. From the trig point beyond the Giant's Grave, the view to the west along the downland escarpment bordering the Vale of Pewsey is exceptional.

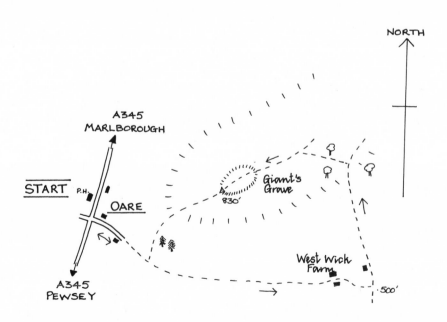

45

The Walk

Turn left at the minor crossroads just south of the White Hart. This quiet lane soon becomes a bridlepath running beneath the southern slopes of Martinsell Hill, the Giant's Grave conspicuous on the hilltop. In ¾ mile, pass through the complex of buildings that make up West Wick Farm, and continue to a junction.

Turn left, and follow a bridlepath as it begins the steady climb towards the hilltop. In ½ mile, at the foot of the escarpment, the path passes through a gateway. Beyond this point, turn left at a junction and climb the steep path onto the downs. Turn left at the top of the climb, pass through a gateway and continue along the hilltop to the Giant's Grave and the trig point on the western tip of the hill. Rainscombe House lies below to the right, whilst the downland escarpment stretches away in the distance.

Descend the far side of the hill, following the fence. When you reach a small spinney, pass through the handgate on the right and continue along the field boundary back to the bridlepath followed out of Oare. A right turn will soon return you to the middle of the village, and the welcoming sight of the White Hart.

⑩ Bishops Cannings
The Crown Inn

Bishops Cannings is a village of thatched cottages, nestling beneath the downs at the western end of the Vale of Pewsey. The tall spire of St Mary the Virgin, 130 ft in height, is a notable landmark for miles around. You may be forgiven for thinking that the church looks a little like Salisbury Cathedral – it is indeed almost a replica in miniature. Both of these religious buildings are cruciform in layout, and are noted for their fine spires. The similarities should come as no surprise, for the Bishops of Salisbury owned the local manorial estates from before Domesday through to 1858. In the shadow of this imposing church stands the red-brick Crown.

This village inn, consisting of public bar, lounge bar and out-sales, has been extensively modernised in recent years. The lounge, for example, has coordinated carpeting, cushions and wallpaper, with a large number of reproduction table-and-chair sets spread throughout its smaller partitioned areas. Equally,the fireplace is no longer functional, but serves as a decorative

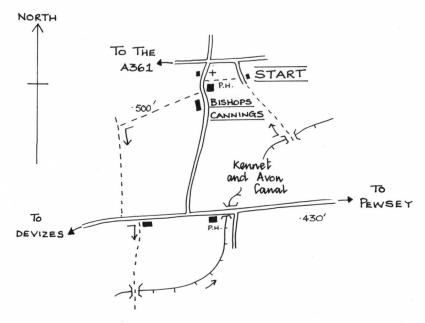

feature. Despite this lack of original features, however, the Crown provides a comfortable and welcoming atmosphere for visitors. Around the walls hang a selection of prints, plates and cigarette cards. The prints featuring the nearby Kennet & Avon Canal will be of particular interest. Youngsters are clearly welcome here and will enjoy the garden to the rear of the inn. Not only does this have a play area, but there is also crazy golf. How much better than keeping restless children cooped up indoors!

The standard menu is divided up into various sections – sandwiches, rolls, salads, steaks, main meals and smaller meals. There is also a children's selection that includes chicken nuggets, pizza and small steaks. A range of specials is displayed on boards in the bar. These might include chicken and mushroom satay, fried potato skins with barbecue sauce, deep-fried Camembert, salmon fishcakes and cheesy potato wedges with ratatouille and salad. The sweets are surely designed to restore those calories lost on the walk – hot chocolate fudge cake, orange fudge cake, treacle sponge and hot apple pie, for example. As this is a Wadworth house, the Devizes-based

brewery that has consistently supported real ale, IPA or 6X should be your natural choice, beers produced from a 92% malt mash. Cider drinkers might prefer to sample a glass of Dry Blackthorn.
Telephone: 01380 86218.

How to get there: Bishops Cannings lies on an unclassified road east of the A361, 3 miles north of Devizes. The inn is by the church.

Parking: There is a car park for patrons alongside the Crown. Roadside parking is also available by the inn and the neighbouring church.

Length of the walk: 3 miles. Map: OS Landranger 173 Swindon and Devizes (inn GR 037641).

From the village, pleasant footpaths are crossed to reach a quiet stretch of the Kennet & Avon Canal. This section of the waterway meanders across the Vale of Pewsey, without a lock between Devizes and Wootton Rivers. Along the way, you will pass the Bridge Inn at Horton, alongside which are moored a colourful array of narrow boats. Throughout the walk, the North Wessex downs form a magnificent backdrop. Wiltshire's highest point, Tan Hill, at 964 ft above sea level is just one landmark to look out for.

The Walk

From the Crown, walk the few yards along the road to the telephone box at the junction with The Estate Yard. Cross the stile on the right just before the telephone box, and make for the stile in the opposite corner of the small field beyond. Cross the middle of the next field to the gateway/gap opposite, beyond which you bear right and follow the hedgerow on the right across a couple of larger fields. Just by some pylons, you join a cross-track. Turn left at this track, which is followed down to the Devizes to Pewsey road, all the while taking in the fine views across the Vale of Pewsey to the downs.

Turn left at the road for just 50 yards, before leaving the road and turning right by a complex of wooden farm buildings. Head across the field next to these buildings to reach Laywood Bridge and the Kennet & Avon Canal. It may be necessary to follow the

49

Kennet and Avon canal.

left-hand edge of the field around to the bridge if the field is cultivated. Cross Laywood Bridge, and follow the towpath to the left.

The canal is followed for over 1 mile as it heads off towards Pewsey. This 15-mile pound must have come as a welcome relief after the rigours of the Caen Hill flight of locks in Devizes. In ¾ mile, the towpath passes beneath a road bridge alongside the Bridge Inn, whilst in another ½ mile the path reaches a swingbridge.

Cross this swingbridge, and follow the track beyond across the fields into Bishops Cannings. The spire of St Mary the Virgin will guide you. When you reach a lane on the edge of the village, continue ahead for just 75 yards before turning left into Church Walk. This path leads into the churchyard, at the far side of which lies the Crown.

Seend Cleeve
The Barge Inn

11

It might be just 5 miles along the Kennet & Avon Canal from Devizes to Seend Cleeve, but the short haul includes a staggering 30 locks. The Barge Inn must have come as something of a blessing to the thirsty bargees! The inn stands on the site of the former Seend Wharf, where as well as ale for the barge-owners, there was stabling and rest for the hauliers' horses.

This is a fine old pub, only recently modernised to make the most of its magnificent waterside location. Crafted of local Bath-stone, and with a fine garden overlooking the canal, it is not difficult to see why the Barge has become one of the area's most popular hostelries. Victorian gas lamps line the water's edge, whilst in summertime hanging baskets and flower tubs and climbing red ivy adorn the inn and its environs. Internally, it is comfortably decorated with oak tables and chairs, and milk churns serving as bar stools. Finely painted flowers with a Victorian feel decorate both the walls and ceiling, a horticultural

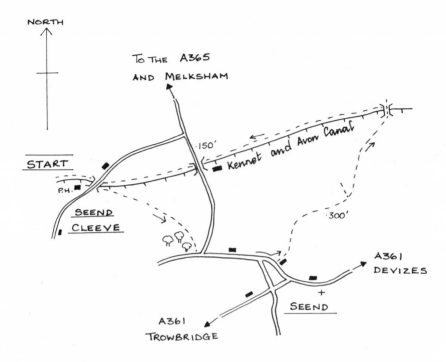

theme that is continued with the bunches of dried flowers that decorate the bar area. On those cold winter evenings, the original fireplace with its black-leaded grate provides welcome warmth.

The range of food available at the Barge has earned it a well-deserved reputation. Snacks might include jacket potatoes, home-made soup, ploughman's lunches, chicken and mushroom pie or scampi, whilst youngsters can choose from their own list of dishes. The dining area overlooking the canal provides customers with a more extensive menu that changes every few weeks. Traditional appetites might enjoy a rack of lamb or sirloin steak, whilst wild mushrooms with green beans, butterbeans, broccoli and sliced almonds in a Provençal sauce will interest more sophisticated palates. The Barge is a Wadworth house, which makes the renowned 6X beer almost obligatory. This famous local brewery has been producing fine ales from its Devizes headquarters since 1885.

Telephone: 01380 823230.

How to get there: 2 miles east of Melksham on the A365 Devizes road, turn south on to an unclassified road signposted to Seend. In just under ½ mile, turn right again along a lane signposted to Seend Cleeve. In a short distance, just after the lane crosses the Kennet & Avon Canal, you will find the Barge Inn on the right-hand side.

Parking: There is a car park for patrons behind the Barge, and room for roadside parking in the vicinity of the inn.

Length of the walk: 2 miles. Map: OS Landranger 173 Swindon and Devizes (inn GR 932613).

Seend Cleeve was a hive of industrial activity in the mid 19th century, with the Great Western Iron Ore Smelting Company extracting and processing the local ore deposits. The hummocky ground alongside the Kennet & Avon at the beginning of the walk marks the site of this enterprise. From the waterway, our steps climb onto a small ridge that stands above the North Wiltshire Clay Vale. This slight elevation brings surprisingly far-ranging views. An easy descent to the canal is followed by a fine section of towpath walking. Locks 19 to 21 lie on this stretch of the waterway – with the Town Lock in nearby Devizes being number 50, you can appreciate why this length of the canal was not flavour of the month with the bargees!

The Walk

Just before the lane crosses the canal on the Barge side of the waterway, cross a stile on the right into an adjoining field. The path is signposted as 'not a canal path'. This field marks the site of the 19th-century iron workings, with the bumpy ground being former spoil tips. Walk alongside the canal for a short distance to lock 19, before bearing slightly to the right and climbing away from the waterway. Aim for a stile in the fence just before a prominent clump of beech trees. Beyond this stile, the field path passes around the left-hand edge of the beech trees to come to another stile in the top corner of the field. Cross this stile, and turn left along a lane to reach a road junction in a matter of yards.

Continue ahead, following the pavement alongside the road signposted to Seend. In 150 yards, turn left onto a quiet side road. In just 25 yards, alongside a red-brick house, turn left

53

Canalside scene at Seend.

again onto a track. This track shortly runs along the top of an open hillside, bringing extensive views across the North Wiltshire countryside. Continue to a junction, where you should be able to spot a five-fingered signpost in the overgrown hedgerow. Turn left, and you will notice a couple of possible paths. The enclosed footpath immediately to the left should be ignored. Instead, cross the stile alongside the neighbouring gateway, and head diagonally downhill across a couple of fields to the canal. There is a clearly visible swingbridge across the waterway, which acts as a landmark.

Cross the swingbridge, and follow the towpath to the left. Just past lock 21, you must leave the waterway to go over the Seend road, beyond which the towpath continues back to the Barge. Pass under the bridge just before you reach the inn, and steps on the right will then bring you up to the road and an excellent watering hole.

12 Bradford-on-Avon
The Three Horseshoes

Originally a 'broad ford' where the river Avon could be crossed, the Saxon town of Bradford-on-Avon rose to prominence as a centre of the West of England woollen trade and has been responsible for the launch of any number of postcards, television programmes, books and magazine features. Several of the old mills survive, fashioned from the same mellow stone that was used so extensively in Georgian Bath. Amidst the architectural delights – which include merchants' houses, a diminutive Saxon church, a lock-up on the Town Bridge and a 14th-century tithe barn – lie scattered a handful of fine old inns. Included in this number is the Three Horseshoes, a town-centre hostelry that exudes a real sense of history.

The comfortable bar areas are furnished with a mixture of high-backed wooden settles and oak tables and chairs. With its dark beams, exposed stonework and open fireplaces, the inn possesses a truly traditional atmosphere. A selection of local photographs, horse yokes and harnesses, copper and brass

The lock-up and the Town Bridge in Bradford-on-Avon.

artefacts complete the picture in this fine old English pub. Outside there is a small beer garden.

The Three Horseshoes offers visitors an excellent choice of well-prepared dishes. The lunchtime menu includes ratatouille, Spanish omelette, kedgeree, and scrambled egg and smoked salmon, as well as a range of sandwiches and ploughman's lunches. Later in the day, a comprehensive range of dishes can be enjoyed in the rear dining area. The evening menu covers starters, grills, fish, home-made dishes, specials and puddings, whilst bar meals are also available. On the main menu you may find, for example, Cajun-style chicken, venison casserole in red wine, pan-fried trout with almonds and chestnut patties in red wine. A choice of good beers is also served, such as Oakhill Bitter, Wadworth 6X, Newquay Steam Bitter and the excellent Broad Oak Bitter from Wickwar. At the end of a delightful walk through the surrounding Avon valley, this is a hostelry where a warm welcome, appetising food and good beer will certainly await you.

Telephone: 01225 865876.

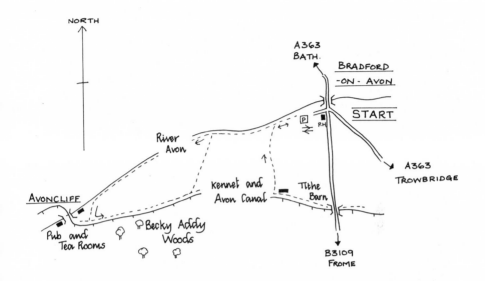

How to get there: Bradford-on-Avon lies on the A363 Bath to Trowbridge road. The Three Horseshoes is in the town centre overlooking the busy junction of the A363 Trowbridge Road with the B3109 Frome Road.

Parking: Bradford-on-Avon station, with its large, free car park, lies immediately to the rear of the Three Horseshoes.

Length of the walk: 3 miles. Map: OS Landranger 173 Swindon and Devizes (inn GR 824607).

This delightful excursion follows both the river Avon and the Kennet & Avon Canal between Bradford-on-Avon, once described as 'a clone of Bath', and neighbouring Avoncliff, which is of particular interest to the industrial archaeologist, being a settlement founded on the local stone and woollen industries. Today the hamlet is dominated by a substantial aqueduct carrying the Kennet & Avon Canal across the Avon. Both river and canal between Bradford and Avoncliff run through the Barton Farm Country Park. Bird-watchers will easily spot the moorhens, coots and mallards that live along the river, but it will take a sharp eye and a quiet step to discover the herons and kingfishers that frequent this part of the valley.

The Walk

Walk to the far end of the station car park in Bradford, and follow the path to the left, down to the river Avon, that runs beneath the railway line. The river bank is literally followed for 1½ miles, all the way to Avoncliff. After ½ mile, the tarmac path bears left to climb up to the Kennet & Avon Canal. At this point, our route lies to the right, leaving the tarmac to follow a field path that runs beside the river.

Just as you reach Avoncliff – marked by the roar of the local weir – the path bears to the left to reach a flight of steps leading up to the canal. A right-turn takes you into the hamlet, where the Cross Guns inn overlooks a quite magnificent aqueduct.

To return to Bradford, follow the canal towpath back to that flight of steps. This time, continue along the towpath for another mile or so until, just before the town's magnificent tithe barn, you follow a short flight of steps on the left down to the river Avon. It is now a simple question of retracing your steps back to the station car park and the Three Horseshoes.

13 Bratton
The Duke

Bratton lies in the shadow of Salisbury Plain, with the downland escarpment rising to the south of the village. The B3098 running from Westbury to West Lavington forms the main street through the village, off which run a series of cottage-lined lanes. The Duke, a brick and tile building, was originally a terrace of three little houses dating from the 18th century, and now houses a public bar, a lounge and a cottage-style restaurant.

Internally, there is a pleasing mixture of plaster and dark wood beams. The lounge bar is comfortably furnished with a number of tables and chairs, and a sofa alongside the fireplace, whilst around the walls hang a mixture of china and rural prints. The restaurant area – the only part of the pub where children are admitted – is well supplied with reproduction dark wood dining furniture. Alongside the inn lies a pleasant beer garden, an ideal spot for youngsters on a warm summer's day.

The extensive menu covers starters, English country dishes, fish, grills, salads and puddings. Starters range from the traditional home-made soup through to the rather more exotic Stilton and port mousse served with toast, whilst among the main courses is Dorset venison in a red wine and port sauce, with pastry topping. Equally enticing would be the two fillets of applewood smoked trout served with a horseradish sauce. Lesser appetites might prefer a more straightforward Wiltshire ham doorstep, a pizza or a cheese ploughman's. There are no special children's dishes, but all items on the menu are available in smaller portions for youngsters. The beers and ales on offer might include Bass or Whitbread Bitter, Ushers Best Bitter or Mole's, the latter from a local brewery based in Melksham, founded in 1982 by ex-Ushers brewer Roger Catté. 'Mole's' comes from his nickname! What could be better than a pint of fine Wiltshire ale quenching one's thirst in the shadow of the Westbury White Horse?

Telephone: 01380 830242.

How to get there: The village of Bratton is 3 miles east of Westbury, on the B3098 West Lavington road. The Duke lies alongside the main road in the centre of the village.

Parking: There is a large car park alongside the Duke, as well as roadside parking in the vicinity of the inn.

Length of the walk: 3 miles. Map: OS Landranger 184 Salisbury and the Plain (inn GR 913523).

Bratton is a spring-line settlement, lying at the scarp foot of Salisbury Plain's northern edge. Hidden in a combe at the foot of the hills is St James' church, decorated with some particularly grisly looking gargoyles. From the village, our route climbs onto the nearby downs, some 750 ft above sea level. The Westbury White Horse and the adjoining Bratton Camp dominate this corner of Salisbury Plain. Extensive views across the Wiltshire countryside are a suitable reward for the effort involved in reaching such a lofty vantage point.

The Walk
From the Duke, walk along the B3098 towards Westbury. In a short distance, turn left into the Butts. At the top of the lane, alongside an old school building, turn right into Upper Garston Lane. In less than 200 yards, at a quiet crossroads, follow the

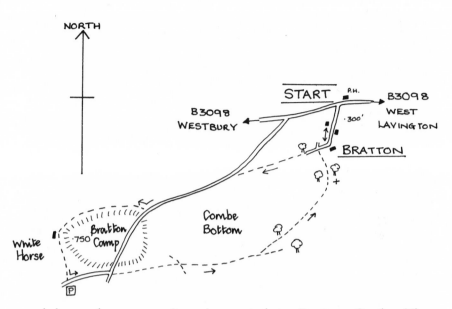

cul-de-sac lane opposite, signposted to Bratton Castle. The tarmac ends in just 50 yards, where you continue along a bridlepath for 400 yards to join the lane that leads to Bratton Castle.

Turn left, and follow this lane as it begins to climb the hillside. The fine views are some compensation for the climb! In 400 yards, a path is signposted on the right as leading back to Bratton. Ignore this path, and continue along the lane for another 300 yards until you see the ramparts of the hill fort on both sides of the road. Turn right at this point, and follow the lower ramparts around the northern edge of the hill fort. The views across the West Wiltshire countryside are quite superb, despite the presence of the nearby Blue Circle cement works with its vast chimney stack.

The path eventually passes directly above the White Horse, where you can literally touch the beast's ear as it protrudes above the level of the hillside! The White Horse was originally cut to commemorate Alfred's battle at Ethandun (nearby Edington?) in 878 AD, where the Danes were defeated. It was supposedly a 'squat ungainly creature with a reptilian tail' until in 1778 a Mr Gee, steward of the local landowner Lord Abingdon, remodelled the horse to today's distinctive design.

61

The Westbury White Horse.

For his efforts he was labelled an 'ignorant destroyer'. A short distance beyond the White Horse, the hilltop path passes through a kissing-gate. A detour to the right will bring you to a convenient topograph, enabling you to interpret the vast view that lies at your feet. The actual route lies directly ahead for 50 yards to the hilltop car park . . . where you may find a convenient ice-cream van.

Take the exit road to the left out of the car park. Shortly, you reach a T-junction – left to Bratton, right a track to White Horse Farm. Our route lies ahead, over the stile on the opposite side of the road. In the next field, drop down to the far right-hand corner. A stile brings you out onto a sunken path. Ahead of you lies the magnificent Combe Bottom, with Bratton away in the distance. Turn right, pass through a gateway and immediately turn left to reach a fence that runs along the hilltop. Walk along the edge of the hill, with the fence to your left, until in 50 yards you reach a gate. Beyond this gate, continue following the fence, which now lies to the right.

In 200 yards, almost imperceptibly, a path bears to the left down the hillside and into the combe. You are aiming for

Bratton church, which is easy to pinpoint. Almost at the foot of the hillside, the path passes through a clump of trees. Once past these trees, aim for the left-hand corner of the field and a stile. Follow the path beyond the stile downhill to reach the western edge of Bratton churchyard, ignoring a couple of stiles on the right. Beyond the churchyard, continue down the steps that lead to a footbridge across the stream. Beyond this stream, the path climbs to reach the quiet crossroads passed at the beginning of the walk. This time, it is a right-turn into Upper Garston Lane, followed by a left-turn into the Butts. You will soon reach the B3098, where the Duke lies just a short distance along to the right.

14 Lower Chute
The Hatchet Inn

Lower Chute lies in a delightfully secluded corner of Wiltshire, within a stone's throw of the Hampshire border and virtually lost along a network of narrow rural byways. It is not the sort of place that visitors would easily stumble across, which makes a visit to the Hatchet something of an expedition! This is a splendid pub, however, and well worth seeking out.

The Hatchet dates back as far as the 16th century, and was formerly a rank of three cottages. With its thatched roof and whitewashed walls, this is one of the most picturesque hostelries in the county. The interior, too, is full of atmosphere and charm. The main lounge bar is dominated by a magnificent open fireplace, where in midwinter a roaring log fire awaits visitors. With its thick beams, patterned carpet, oak tables, wheelback and Captain's chairs, this is an inn where you will be more than happy to while away an hour or two. Alongside the fireplace sits an old iron kettle, together with a pot and ladle, whilst around the lounge is a collection of copper and brass, and a number of interesting prints.

The bar menu changes frequently, but will never disappoint. Examples of the dishes are spaghetti bolognaise, steak and kidney pie, lamb Madras and local game. Vegetarians are well catered for, and could find spinach and tomato lasagne or cauliflower and courgette bake to their liking. At lunchtimes, ploughman's, rolls and sandwiches are also available. Good beers – perhaps Wadworth 6X, Adnams Bitter, Bass or Charrington IPA – are always on offer. Children are welcome in the eating areas, although youngsters would in all probability prefer to spend their time outside in the open air. There is a side lawn with a small play area, a front terrace with picnic benches, as well as plenty of shady tree cover. All-in-all a quite superb inn, with plenty of internal charm and a handsome exterior.

Telephone: 01264 730229.

How to get there: Not the easiest of inns to find! Follow the A342 Devizes to Andover road to the eastern edge of Ludgershall, where an unclassified lane is signposted to Chute. As you approach Chute, the signposts begin to differentiate between Upper Chute and Lower Chute. Follow the signs to the Lower version, and you will find the thatched Hatchet in the centre of the small village.

Parking: There is a gravelled car park at the Hatchet for patrons. There is also room for roadside parking, with care, in the vicinity of the inn, particularly along the lane by the village green and war memorial.

Length of the walk: 3½ miles. Map: OS Landranger 185 Winchester and Basingstoke (inn GR 312532).

This is a landscape of woodland and tree cover, with well maintained windbreaks, copses and plantations. From Lower Chute and Chute Standen, a lonely bridlepath climbs the hillside to Chute Causeway, at one time part of the Roman road from Winchester to Mildenhall, which ran along the hilltop over 800 ft above sea level. The views from this lofty vantage point are quite magnificent, extending across the wooded combes and hillsides of the extreme south-east of Wiltshire. From Chute Causeway, the

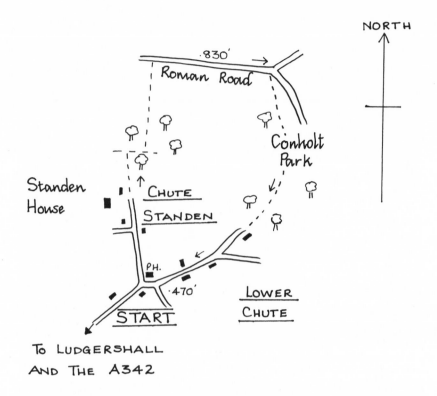

return to Lower Chute runs through Conholt Park, part of the estate of the nearby Conholt House, which dates from the early 19th century.

The Walk

With your back to the Hatchet, follow the road to the right for just a few yards to a junction. Keep right at the junction, and follow the lane signposted to Chute Standen and Upper Chute. In ½ mile, at the junction in Chute Standen, keep straight ahead along the lane signposted as a 'No Through Road'.

Follow this lane past Standen House and on to a red-brick bungalow on the left. Continue beyond this bungalow, the lane now having reverted to a grassy bridlepath. This path climbs for 400 yards to a junction with another bridlepath, where you turn right. In a little way, this path bears to the left and climbs for

The village green, Lower Chute.

¾ mile to the metalled lane shown on the OS sheets as 'Chute Causeway – Roman Road'.

Turn right, and follow this lane across the hilltop for ¾ mile. This is high ground, running at well over 800 ft, with the views to the north dominated by the hill fort high on Fosbury Hill. The fort's ramparts are clearly visible. At the junction with the Andover road, look out for a stile alongside a gate on the right. Cross this stile into Conholt Park.

On the wooden step of the stile is a waymark. Cross the field to the fence opposite, in the direction pointed out by the waymark. Here you will find a second stile and waymarker. Cross this stile, and walk in the direction of the arrow to the fence opposite and yet another stile! In the next – much larger – field, head downhill to a gateway and a cattle grid. Once again, a waymark points the general direction. Beyond the cattle grid, follow the right-hand field boundary across the next field. Almost at the far side of this, where the field has narrowed as tree cover closes in on both sides, cross a stile on the right beside a gate.

Follow the track beyond this stile onto a lane, and continue ahead past a row of estate cottages to a road junction. Turn right, and follow the main road back into Lower Chute. At the junction by the village war memorial, turn right back to the Hatchet.

⑮ Upper Woodford
The Bridge Inn

The river Avon between Amesbury and Salisbury flows through perhaps the most idyllic and unspoilt valley in Wiltshire. Along the river lie a number of delightful villages – including Lower, Middle and Upper Woodford – characterised by thatched cottages, ancient churches and fine manor houses. The Bridge Inn at Upper Woodford actually fronts onto the clear waters of the Avon, with the beer garden overlooking the river – perhaps the best-located of all Wiltshire's pub gardens – being as popular with the local duck population as with patrons! The inn takes its name from the nearby bridge, a construction unique to the Avon as it flows through Wiltshire and Hampshire to the sea at Christchurch. It is a brick structure, with stone piers and iron railings.

The inn's black window shutters contrast effectively with its whitewashed walls, presenting a pleasing aspect when viewed from the garden alongside the river. Internally, there is a single main bar, off which lie a restaurant and a games room. The dark-green and cream paintwork, patterned carpets, pine tables and wooden armchairs give the interior a comfortable feel. This is further enhanced by an extensive collection of prints and pictures, together with various china and copper artefacts.

A full bar menu is available, with a selection of dishes displayed on a blackboard in the bar. Examples are king prawns, Bridge ploughman's, paella, seafood platter and Wiltshire pie, this last dish consisting of sausage meat, stuffing, apple and cider in a shortcrust pastry. Incidentally, the Bridge ploughman's also offers a slice of this delicious local pie. An excellent range of rolls and sandwiches are also on offer, should your appetite unexpectedly fail you. As this is a Gibbs Mew pub it almost beholds you to sample one of the Salisbury brewery's quite exceptional beers. The Wiltshire Bitter and the Salisbury Best Bitter come particularly recommended, as does The Bishop's Tipple. This last beer is especially strong – with an ABV of about 6.6% – so if you are driving it is as well to purchase a couple of bottles for home consumption!

Telephone: 01722 782323.

How to get there: An unclassified road follows the Avon valley between Amesbury and Salisbury. Upper Woodford is on this byway, just 4 miles south of Amesbury. The Bridge Inn lies alongside the road in the centre of the village, opposite the Avon.

Parking: There is a car park for patrons opposite the inn, alongside the garden. There is also room for careful roadside parking in the vicinity of the inn.

Length of the walk: 2½ miles. Map: OS Landranger 184 Salisbury and the Plain (inn GR 123372).

The chalk stream, delightful brick and thatch cottages, old mills and fertile farmland provide a backdrop to this fine excursion in a beautiful corner of Wiltshire. From Upper Woodford, there is a steep climb on to the hilltops to the east of the river. The reward is a fine vantage point with views across the Avon and towards the neighbouring village of Great Durnford. The path descends into Great Durnford, described in a local guidebook as 'a delightful village of old-world cottages and flowering gardens spilling over the roadside

Attractive cottages along the route in Great Durnford.

verges'. St Andrew's church dating from early Norman times, is well worth a short detour. The return to Upper Woodford is by way of Durnford Mill and a path that follows an elevated course above the Avon.

The Walk

Cross the bridge over the Avon, and continue along the road ahead for 300 yards. At the first junction, turn left along the lane signposted to Great Durnford. In ¼ mile, there are good views of the river as the lane runs alongside the Avon. Continue along the lane until, just 50 yards before the Great Durnford road sign, a permissive path climbs the steep slope on the right-hand side. If you have gone as far as a small chalk quarry, you have gone too far!

Turn right, and climb directly up the hillside for 50 yards, before bearing to the right to continue along the path as it climbs more gently up the hilltop. Pause for breath to enjoy the fine views below of the Avon valley. At the top of the hill, the path bears to the left to run along the edge of the hilltop. Continue following the waymarked path through scrubland until you come to a fence that runs up the hillside. Follow the

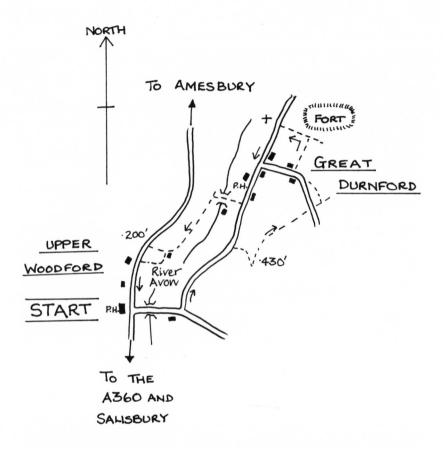

fence ahead, continuing along the hilltop path. Eventually, the path leaves the scrubland to enter a field on the right. Follow the left-hand hedgerow to the corner of this field, pass through the scrub on the left into the next field, and continue along its left-hand boundary to the corner of the field and a quiet lane.

Pass through the gateway across the road, and immediately turn left to follow the edge of the field downhill towards Great Durnford. The hummocky ground that the field path passes through is shown on the OS sheet as an ancient field system. At the foot of the hill, just before reaching the village, cross a stile on the left and continue following the lane into Great Durnford.

Shortly before the first dwelling on the right, a bungalow, cross a stile alongside a gate into a small field. Continue to the gateway opposite, beyond which you follow the fence uphill across a couple of fields to reach a track. Above the track lies Ogbury Fort – which can be explored with the help of the OS sheet. Our route lies to the left, with the track being followed down into Great Durnford.

When you reach the main street in the village, the lane opposite leads to the church. Our route continues to the left, along the main street until, 100 yards past the Black Horse, we turn right into a bridlepath signposted to Durnford Mill. Cross the wooden footbridges alongside the mill, across the sluices, to reach the far side of the Avon. Here the path reaches a junction. Turn left, to follow the path that climbs gently uphill to reach an elevated position above the river.

Continue ahead, ignoring a turning to the right, with the path running alongside the trees above the river. This enclosed path soon heads away from the river to head back to Upper Woodford. When you reach a junction with another track, with a tennis court directly opposite, turn left. This track passes between paddocks and old farm buildings to join the lane leading back to the Bridge. Turn left, and it is just a few minutes walk back to the inn.

16 Great Wishford
The Royal Oak

The inn sign on the Royal Oak carries the odd-sounding phrase, 'Grovely, Grovely, Grovely and All Grovely.' This is a reference to the annual Oak Apple Day festivities, when villagers claim their right to collect 'all kinde of deade snappinge woode, boughes and stickes' from Grovely Wood, the local forest. May 29th, the day of this ancient right, is understandably a busy day for the local hostelry!

The Royal Oak, a red-brick building bedecked with a magnificent creeper, dates from the 17th century. At the front of the inn is a comfortable bar, which leads through to a large dining area created from a former stable block. Bare boards, wood-panelling, dark oak beams and wooden settles give the bar a traditional feel, which is complemented by a couple of fine open fireplaces. Roaring log fires provide welcome warmth in the winter months. Around the walls are displayed a number of rural artefacts, including a collection of stirrups and a display case of fishing flies. Cartographers will be attracted by an old

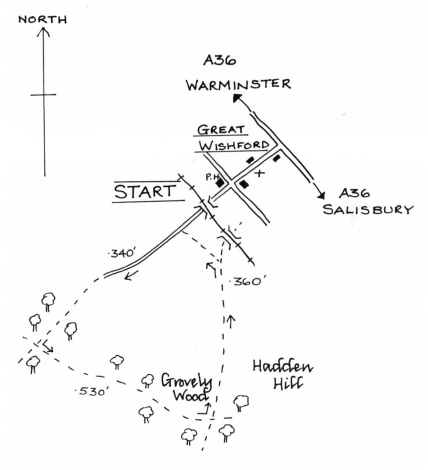

map of the city of Salisbury.

The inn has earned a well-deserved reputation for the quality of its food. As well as the menu listing the standard fare – ploughman's lunches, sandwiches, soups, salads and jacket potatoes – there are no fewer than five boards displaying an ever-changing variety of dishes. To whet your appetite, examples are smoked trout pâté, wild boar and apple sausages, pheasant and vegetable pie, home-made faggots in onion gravy and surf and turf. This last dish is an intriguing mixture of steak and king prawns. Imaginative vegetarian selections and a good range of children's meals are on offer, too. The sweets are

St Giles' church, Great Wishford.

equally appealing, and include lemon lush pie and death by chocolate. Children are welcome in the eating areas of the Royal Oak, as well as on the lawn beside the inn, where there are a number of picnic tables. The real ales on offer are Courage Directors and Best Bitter. A stroll through Grovely Wood, with refreshment at this delightful hostelry, is an idyllic way to pass a few hours at any time of year.
Telephone: 01722 790229.

How to get there: Great Wishford lies just off the A36 Salisbury to Warminster trunk road, 3 miles north of Wilton. Follow the signposted turning across the river Wylye, past St Giles' church, and on to a minor crossroads overlooked by the Royal Oak.

Parking: There is a car park for patrons to the rear of the Royal Oak. There is also room for careful roadside parking in the vicinity of the inn.

Length of the walk: 4 miles. Map: OS Landranger 184 Salisbury and the Plain (inn GR 077355).

A relaxing walk from the attractive village of Great Wishford, deep in the Wylye valley between Warminster and Salisbury, up onto the wooded hills to the south-west. Here our steps pass through the ancient forest of Grovely Wood, where a particularly impressive avenue of copper beech trees will certainly catch the eye. This avenue lies along the course of the Roman road that ran from Salisbury to the West Country. The bridlepath that descends the downs back into Great Wishford brings extensive views across the Wylye valley towards Salisbury Plain. Throughout, the rights-of-way are clearly defined and the gradients generally slight.

The Walk
Follow the lane alongside the Royal Oak, that goes underneath the railway bridge carrying the Bristol to Southampton railway. This estate road runs along the bottom of a dry valley, all the while heading in the direction of Grovely Wood. In 1 mile, the lane enters the woodland, where a sign announces to visitors that this is part of the Wilton Estates. Climb through the woods for ½ mile to a junction, where a telegraph pole bears the legend 'all dogs must be kept on a lead'. Turn left at this

junction, to follow an estate lane through a magnificent beech avenue.

Continue ahead for 1 mile, with the copper beeches lining your route all the while. Alongside a coniferous plantation, a well-defined bridlepath crosses the estate road at a slight angle. Turn left at this junction, and follow the bridlepath until it emerges from Grovely Wood onto the open downland of Hadden Hill. Magnificent views open up across the Wylye valley.

Continue along this enclosed bridlepath as it descends the hillside back into Great Wishford. On the edge of the village, a short distance before a railway bridge, turn left onto an enclosed track. Follow this track for 200 yards back to the lane followed at the start of the walk. A right turn takes you under the railway and back to the Royal Oak.

⓱ Corton
The Dove Inn

Two parallel roads run either side of the river Wylye between Warminster and Salisbury. The A36 trunk road, choked with heavy lorries heading to and from Southampton, runs to the north of the river. Across the valley runs a meandering byway, almost set in a time-warp, that passes through a number of sleepy, quintessentially English villages. Corton, with its stone, brick and flint cottages, lies on the south side of the valley. Tucked away off the village's main street is the Dove, a delightful stone inn with courtyard parking to the front and an attractive garden behind.

The front door to the inn opens directly into the lounge bar, with several interconnecting rooms away on the left. The wooden flooring and the timber bar provide a suitably rustic feel to the Dove, where settles, cushioned stools and a good number of tables and chairs provide every comfort for patrons. Around the walls are displayed a number of local paintings, prints and photographs, with old cider pots and bottles adding

79

further elements of interest. The wintertime log fire in the brick fireplace completes the picture. All-in-all, a good deal of thought has gone into creating a homely feel, giving the inn, as one guidebook noted, 'the feel of a private residence'. It is an excellent little pub, with a warm and welcoming atmosphere.

The day's menu is chalked up in the lounge. This could include home-made tomato soup, local game pie, ploughman's lunches, burgers made from 100% ground beef, and beef and vegetable stew with a jacket potato. Altogether very traditional well-prepared fare. Examples of the sweets are apple and cinnamon pie and lemon sorbet. Children are welcome in the eating areas of the Dove, as well as in the lovely garden. Real ale enthusiasts will find much to their liking here, too. The range of beers does change frequently in this freehouse, but if I tell you that the selection could include Anna Valley Bitter, Hop Back Summer Lightning or Oakhill Bitter, you will get the picture. Hop Back is a Salisbury-based brewery whose Summer Lightning brew has won CAMRA awards.

Telephone: 01985 850109.

How to get there: If approaching from Warminster town centre, follow the main road towards Heytesbury and the town's bypass. This is in fact the old A36, reclassified as the B3414 since the bypass was built. On the edge of the town, turn right onto the B3095 for Sutton Veny. Corton lies on the unclassified road that runs through the Wylye valley between Sutton Veny and Wylye. As you reach the village, turn onto a lane signposted 'Corton – No Through Road'. This lane immediately forks by a small green. If you follow the right fork, the Dove is just a few yards down the road on the left-hand side.

Parking: There is a small courtyard in front of the Dove where patrons may park their vehicles. Just by the inn is a small green where there is room for roadside parking.

Length of the walk: 3½ miles. Map: OS Landranger 184 Salisbury and the Plain (inn GR 935405).

The Wylye valley is one of the most beautiful parts of Wiltshire. A clear chalk stream, villages dotted with stone, brick and thatched cottages,

The Little Manor, Corton.

downland on the horizon, ancient churches – the sort of landscape that every expatriate Englishman must constantly dream about. This walk explores a small corner of the valley, taking in the villages of Corton, Heytesbury and Knook. Along the way, we pass a fine watermill, delightful 18th-century almshouses in Heytesbury, and the old church of St Margaret in Knook. For lengthy stretches of the walk, the river is our constant companion. A peaceful stroll across the English countryside, with not even the slightest of gradients.

The Walk

Head back to the unclassified road that runs down through the Wylye valley, and turn right towards Warminster. In just a few yards, cross a stile on the right to follow a signposted footpath across an open field to a stile opposite. Beyond this stile, the path borders a nursery to reach another stile. Cross this stile and continue along the field boundary ahead. Halfway along the edge of the field, cross a stile on the right and continue following the opposite side of the field boundary to the corner of the field. Here there is a stile, beyond which an enclosed path passes beneath the Bristol to Southampton railway.

A short distance beyond the railway bridge, the path bears left

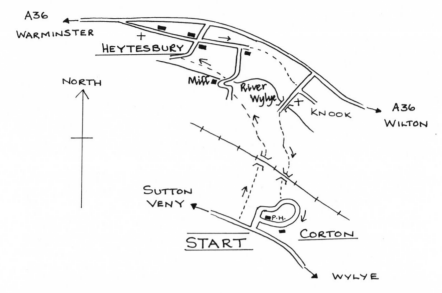

to cross a fence by way of a single-step stile. Follow the right-hand field boundary across the next field – it soon becomes an enclosed path – to a stile, beyond which the path continues to a lane running from Corton to Heytesbury.

Turn right, and follow the lane around through the complex of buildings that make up Heytesbury Mill. Just beyond the mill, the road crosses the river Wylye. Once over the river, turn left to follow a footpath alongside it. The path soon enters an open field, where you follow the left-hand fence beside the Wylye to the far corner. Beyond this point, an enclosed path continues besides the Wylye towards Heytesbury. You shortly pass a seat by the river. In just 25 yards, at a junction, turn right and continue up to a crossroads. Across the road are the local almshouses in Heytesbury, known as the Hospital of St John and St Katharine.

Turn right along Park Street, at one time the busy A36 until Heytesbury received its bypass. In 600 yards, where Park Street bears to the right, continue ahead along a cul-de-sac. Where this road ends – it is the truncated former A36 – continue along a footpath that runs beside the A36(T). In just 25 yards, turn right along a signposted footpath that follows the left-hand side of a field before passing into an area of coniferous trees. This path continues above the Wylye for just under ½ mile into Knook, the path leaving the river about 100 yards before the village.

As you enter the village, turn right at a crossroads to follow a lane past St Margaret's church and the neighbouring manor, down to a footbridge over the Wylye. Cross the river, ignore a stile on the right, and continue onto an open field. Bear half-left and follow a raised field path across a couple of fields – the well-worn route is very clear. At the far side of the second field, cross a stile on the right to reach an enclosed path.

This path continues for ½ mile back to Corton, passing under the Southampton railway en route. As you enter the village, you pass the Old Chapel on the left. Just beyond this now private residence, turn left at a road junction to follow a lane around through the village back to the Dove. Just before the inn, look out for the Little Manor on the right, complete with its well.

⑱ Kilmington
The Red Lion Inn

The Red Lion can boast a fair history. Originally a farmhouse, it was subsequently converted to a pub by the local landowner. This provided a meeting place for the hard-working labourers on his estate. Later still, it served as a drovers' inn and posthouse for the coach route running from the West Country to Salisbury, a route this walk follows onto White Sheet Hill.

This sense of history is evident inside the inn, with its flagstone floor, its fine old beams and a pair of open fireplaces – complete with roaring log fires in the winter months. Window seats and a black settle add a pleasant feel to the bar area, along with brasses, china and photographs. Weather permitting, food and liquid refreshment can be enjoyed in the inn's rear garden, with its views extending eastwards. Children are welcome in the garden and the eating area of the Red Lion until 9 pm.

A range of traditional bar snacks are available – soup, jacket potatoes, sandwiches, ploughman's lunches and salads, for example. If your excursion onto the nearby downs has left you with a more substantial appetite, try one of the delicious pies on the menu. These include steak and kidney, game, lamb and apricot and a particularly tempting fish pie. To accompany your meal, a choice of fine real ales is always available. These might include Butcombe Bitter, Bass and Marston's Pedigree, and a strong farmhouse cider is also served. The *Good Pub Guide* got it exactly right when it described the Red Lion as 'a wonderfully unpretentious, friendly and unspoilt pub.' Surrounded by exceptional walking country this historic hostelry is well worth a visit.

Telephone: 01985 844263.

How to get there: The Red Lion at Kilmington (actually 1 mile from the village) lies on the B3092 Mere road, 8 miles south of Frome. The National Trust's Stourhead Estate lies just ½ mile south of the inn.

Parking: There is a car park attached to the Red Lion for the use of patrons. There are also a couple of laybys alongside the inn on the B3092.

Field path from White Sheet Hill.

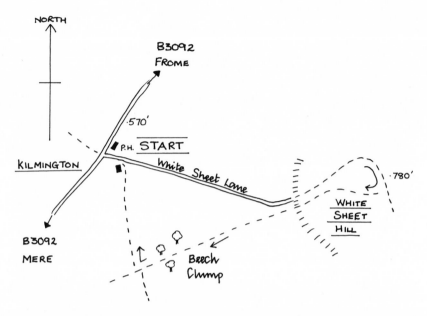

Length of the walk: 2½ miles. Map: OS Landranger 183 Yeovil and Frome (inn GR 787353).

A magnificent circuit that climbs onto the NT's White Sheet Hill property. This is a large area of unimproved chalk downland, home to a number of archaeological sites, among them a hill fort, a cross-ridge dyke and a causewayed enclosure dating from 3000 BC. With the plough and chemical fertiliser banned on the hilltop, an abundance of flora awaits the visitor in the spring and summer months, including cowslips, orchids, vetches and campanulas, which in turn attract such rare butterflies as the chalk-hill blue. The views are quite special, too, extending westwards to the Stourhead Estate and Alfred's Tower away on the Somerset border.

The Walk

Follow the byway – White Sheet Lane – that runs alongside the Red Lion in the direction of White Sheet Hill. In ¾ mile, the lane begins its climb onto the hilltop and passes a gravelled parking area on the right-hand side. Continue past this parking area, the lane now becoming an unmetalled track.

At the top of the hill, the track bears to the right, with magnificent views opening up in all directions. In a short

86

distance, you will pass a NT information board on the right-hand side. This details both the natural and ancient history of the White Sheet Hill site. A few yards past the information board, cross a stile on the right-hand side into the site enclosure. Continue directly ahead to the edge of the hillside, where a far-ranging vista across the Wiltshire countryside awaits you. The nearby Stourhead Estate with its magnificent woodland setting is but one landmark.

Having enjoyed this fine outlook, follow the edge of the hilltop to the right. You will soon meet a fence that runs down the hillside to your left. Cross the stile, and follow the fence downhill until you reach another stile that leads into the gravelled parking area passed earlier. Continue straight ahead, along a bridlepath that follows the right-hand boundary of a couple of fields before reaching a fine beech copse.

Some 100 yards beyond this copse, alongside the second gate you reach on the right-hand side, you will find a stile. Cross this, and follow the left-hand field boundary across the next two fields. Just beyond a thatched cottage at the far corner of the second field, pass through a handgate and continue to the right for a few yards to return to White Sheet Lane. A left turn brings you back to the Red Lion.

19 Ansty
The Maypole Inn

The village of Ansty lays claim to England's tallest maypole, a quite massive 96 ft in height. Fashioned from Douglas fir, this maypole stands in the middle of the street right outside the village inn, which is appropriately named after what has been a feature of village life in this corner of Wiltshire since the 15th century. The Maypole inn was originally built in 1825 to serve as an alehouse for workers on the local Wardour Estate. Today, it is a somewhat more sophisticated hostelry, with increasing emphasis upon its fine food. Built of stone, brick and flint, this white-shuttered building provides a suitable focal point in the centre of the village, alongside the local manor.

Inside there is a bar, dining area and small restaurant. Dark-green hessian walls are decorated with old local photographs, drawings and prints, whilst scattered around the bar are a large number of traditional cider pots. With high-back wooden settles, dark wood tables, open fire and spindleback chairs, a most traditional air pervades this compact and friendly inn.

Whatever your taste in food, there will surely be something to satisfy your appetite at the Maypole. The dishes include lighter snacks, such as sandwiches or jacket potatoes, more substantial topside of beef or lamb chops, and the very imaginative vegetable tortilla or vegetarian nut roast in a tomato and red wine sauce. There is also a special three-course lunchtime menu. The choices on this could be home-made soup, duck pâté and orange or crispy coated baby sweetcorn, among the starters. Main dishes might be fresh fish fillet, grilled pork chop, vegetable curry or chicken cordon bleu, whilst the sweets could include roly poly pudding and chocolate biscuit cake. To satisfy your thirst, good beers and ales are always available. Butcombe Bitter and Wadworth 6X are normally served, as well as, perhaps, Fuller's London Pride. The inn also offers patrons a good selection of wines.

Telephone: 01747 870607.

How to get there: Ansty lies just off the A30, west of Salisbury, between Wilton and Shaftesbury. The Maypole lies in the centre of the village, ½ mile north of the A30.

Parking: There is a car park at the Maypole for patrons, as well as room for roadside parking in the vicinity of the inn.

Length of the walk: 3 miles. Map: OS Landranger 184 Salisbury and the Plain (inn GR 955264).

Ansty contains those fundamental ingredients that make for the archetypal English village — a picturesque church, a manor house, a duckpond, the local maypole and a fine hostelry. The village is the focal point of the local Wardour Estate, rich agricultural land with a large acreage of woodland thrown in for good measure. This walk explores the estate to the west of the village, where in the heart of High Wood we find Old Wardour Castle. Its hexagonal courtyard is a design unique in Britain, and was inspired by similar constructions across the Channel. A quite beautiful walk, in a secluded and little-known corner of Wiltshire.

The Walk

Continue along the narrow lane west of the Maypole for 200 yards until you reach a very minor crossroads. Immediately past

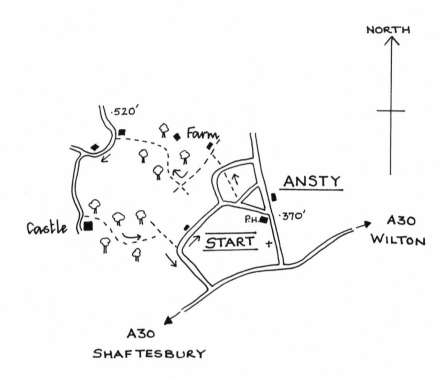

NORTH

·520'

Farm

ANSTY

Castle

P.H. ·370'

START

A30
WILTON

A30
SHAFTESBURY

this crossroads, go through a gate on the right-hand side into open fields. In the first field, cross to the stile opposite. In a boggy second field, aim for the stile beneath the oak tree opposite, and in a third field aim for the gate halfway down the opposite hedgerow. This brings you to a quiet lane.

Turn left for just 20 yards, before going through a gate on the right-hand side. This brings you to a wide grassy track, enclosed by wooden fencing. Do not follow the obvious course along this track, however. Instead, climb the wooden fence and bear half-right towards a stile that leads into an area of woodland. Follow the path beyond this stile through the trees until, in 150 yards, you reach a cross-track. A cottage lies a short distance down to the right.

Turn left, and follow this enclosed track for 400 yards until it enters Twelve Acre Copse. Just inside the copse, you reach a crossroads. Turn right, and take a path along the edge of the woodland above Squalls Farm. Follow the path as it bears to the left and continues to a quiet country lane, ignoring any side turns.

Turn left, and follow the lane uphill through High Wood, enjoying the extensive views to the west. In 200 yards, alongside an isolated cottage, turn left at a junction to follow the access drive signposted to the castle. This lane continues along to the car park beside Old Wardour Castle. Turn left through the parking area, and follow the path uphill by the entrance to this ancient fortification. The woodland path continues uphill, beneath an archway, before leaving the woods and continuing as an enclosed path across open countryside. Away to the right, fine views of the downland above Fovant and Ansty open up.

At the far side of the open fields, the path re-enters Twelve Acre Copse. Two cross-tracks are reached in quick succession. Follow the second of these to the right for 350 yards until you reach another quiet lane. Turn left, and follow this lane through Ansty Coombe and back into Ansty, ignoring a couple of left turns en route. It is close on ½ mile back to the Maypole.

Old Wardour Castle.

91

🔵20 **Bishopstone**
The White Hart

The Ebble is one of those delightful chalk streams that flows into the Avon at Salisbury. It carves a course through the downs to the west of the city, providing a handy living for several local cress growers and trout farmers. Bishopstone is but one of the attractive villages that lie alongside the Ebble, villages where thatch and brick-and-flint form the traditional building materials.

The White Hart lies alongside the main thoroughfare in the village. The local brick has been lost beneath whitewashed plaster, which does give the inn a bright and cheery appearance. Internally, the White Hart has been the subject of considerable modernisation in recent years. The comfortable bar area is furnished with polished table-and-chair sets and sofa seating, and is carpeted throughout. Not surprisingly, visitors are asked to leave muddy footwear at the door! With wood-panelled walls, beams and a brick fireplace, brass and copperware, the inn provides a homely welcome for visitors.

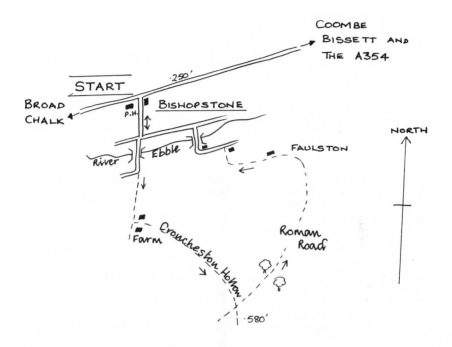

Wholesome portions of traditional pub fare fill the bar menu. Home-made soup, pâté and garlic bread, ploughman's lunches and sandwiches are all available, as are a variety of steak and fish dishes. Local trout from the Ebble could well prove a tempting option. Hearty appetites might also enjoy chicken curry, steak and kidney pie, filled jacket potatoes, omelettes and vegetable or meat lasagne. There are also a range of hot snacks that include burgers, fish fingers and chicken nuggets. A variety of sweets are available too, including the ever-popular home-made apple pie. The White Hart's restaurant has its own extensive menu.

The inn is owned by Gibbs Mew, the Salisbury-based brewery that has been brewing on its current site in the city since 1866. The excellent beers on offer here include Wiltshire Bitter and Salisbury Best Bitter, as well as Tetley Bitter and Guinness. Of equal interest will be the large number of fruit wines available, believed to be the best selection in the area. Youngsters are welcome in the eating areas of the White Hart, along with the restaurant, as well as in the inn's large garden and patio area.

The dovecote in Bishopstone.

There is also an outside play area, where excess energy can be suitably channelled!
Telephone: 01722 780244.

How to get there: Bishopstone is on an unclassified road in the Ebble valley, south-west of Salisbury, midway between Coombe Bissett and Broad Chalke. The White Hart lies on this road in the centre of the village.

Parking: There is a large car park for patrons, to the rear of the White Hart, as well as roadside parking in Butt Lane alongside the inn.

Length of the walk: 3 miles. Map: OS Landranger 184 Salisbury and the Plain (inn GR 068258).

From the Ebble valley, with its cress beds and luxuriant meadows, this walk climbs high onto the downs to the south of Bishopstone. Our steps follow a couple of ancient byways – Croucheston Hollow onto the hilltop, and the Roman road running from Old Sarum to Badbury Rings back into Bishopstone. The views are quite exceptional, extending across the hill-country that lies along the Wiltshire-Dorset border.

The Walk

Follow Butt Lane alongside the White Hart down to a junction, where you turn right into The Alley. In a short distance, just past the Three Horseshoes, turn left along Bridge Road. This road takes you across the Ebble, with cress beds bordering both sides of the highway. Continue along the road – it reverts to a farm track beyond the village – until you reach a complex of farm buildings in about 400 yards.

Turn left, and follow the ancient byway shown as Croucheston Hollow on the OS map. The track passes through the farm buildings before climbing onto the downs. Initially, this is a concrete farm track, which soon reverts to a chalk bridlepath. Fine views soon open up across the Ebble valley. It is a climb of 300 ft onto the hilltop, followed by almost ½ mile of level walking as the bridlepath follows the left-hand hedgerow across the open downland. Look out for a handgate on the left, at a point where a dry valley stretches away on the right-hand side.

Pass through this handgate, and cross the open field ahead, keeping some yards to the left of the raised hump – a reservoir – in the middle of the field. Aim for a gate at the far left-hand end of the fence at the opposite side of the field. Pass through this gateway, and turn immediately to the left, following a sunken path along the edge of the field back downhill towards Bishopstone. This is the course of the old Roman road running towards Old Sarum. In 400 yards, alongside a row of beech trees, the path reaches a gateway. Continue following the bridlepath downhill beyond this gate for over ½ mile, to a point where the path bears to the left to pass alongside a group of old brick-and-flint farm buildings shown on the maps as Faulston. About 150 yards past the farm buildings, the track bears left. At this point, cross the gate on the right to follow an enclosed path past some cottages out onto a lane.

Turn left along this lane, which soon passes a magnificent dovecote attached to Faulston House. The lane bears to the right alongside the house, before crossing the Ebble and reaching a road junction. Turn left along Netton Street and, in 250 yards, right into Butt Lane which leads back to the White Hart.